The Story of
Saint Valentine

Every year on February 14, we celebrate a special day – Valentine's Day – by giving and receiving special cards to and from people we care about. But do you know why we celebrate this way and who Saint Valentine was? Let's find out!

In 269 AD, the Roman Empire ruled the world—but it was in trouble! Enemy tribes were invading all along the border. Emperor Claudius needed to stop the invasion, but he had one big problem.

Claudius needed a bigger army. There just weren't enough soldiers to send into battle. Then he had an idea! "I will send messengers throughout the land asking for young men to join the army," he thought to himself. To his disappointment, very few young men joined. They knew the emperor expected them to stay in the army for 25 years. That was a long time!

When the emperor realized that no one was joining his army, he got very angry. "I will write a new law!" he growled. "There will be no more weddings in Rome. No one can get married until I get more men in my army!"

The people were shocked and heartbroken. What could they do?

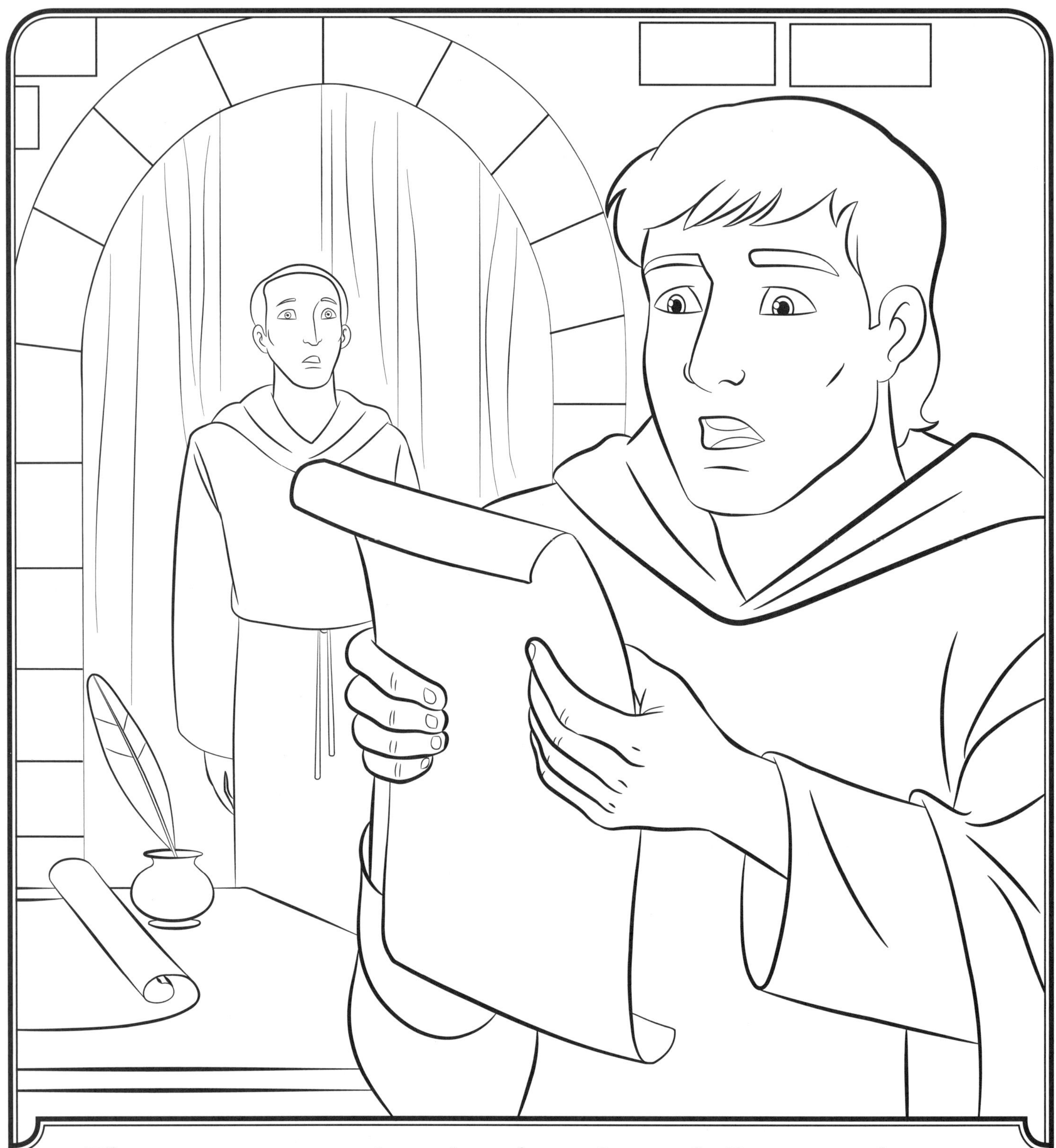

There was a priest in the city of Rome who was also saddened by the news. His name was Valentinus. "Marriage is God's idea," Valentinus told his helper, Marius. "I may go to prison for disobeying the law, but I have to do what I know is right!"

So Valentinus began to work in secret under the cover of night. Deep in the woods, he would meet with couples who were ready for marriage and perform a marriage ceremony for them.

Soon the news of a priest disobeying the law came to Claudius. “How dare anyone defy my laws!” screamed the angry emperor. “Bring this rebel to me!”

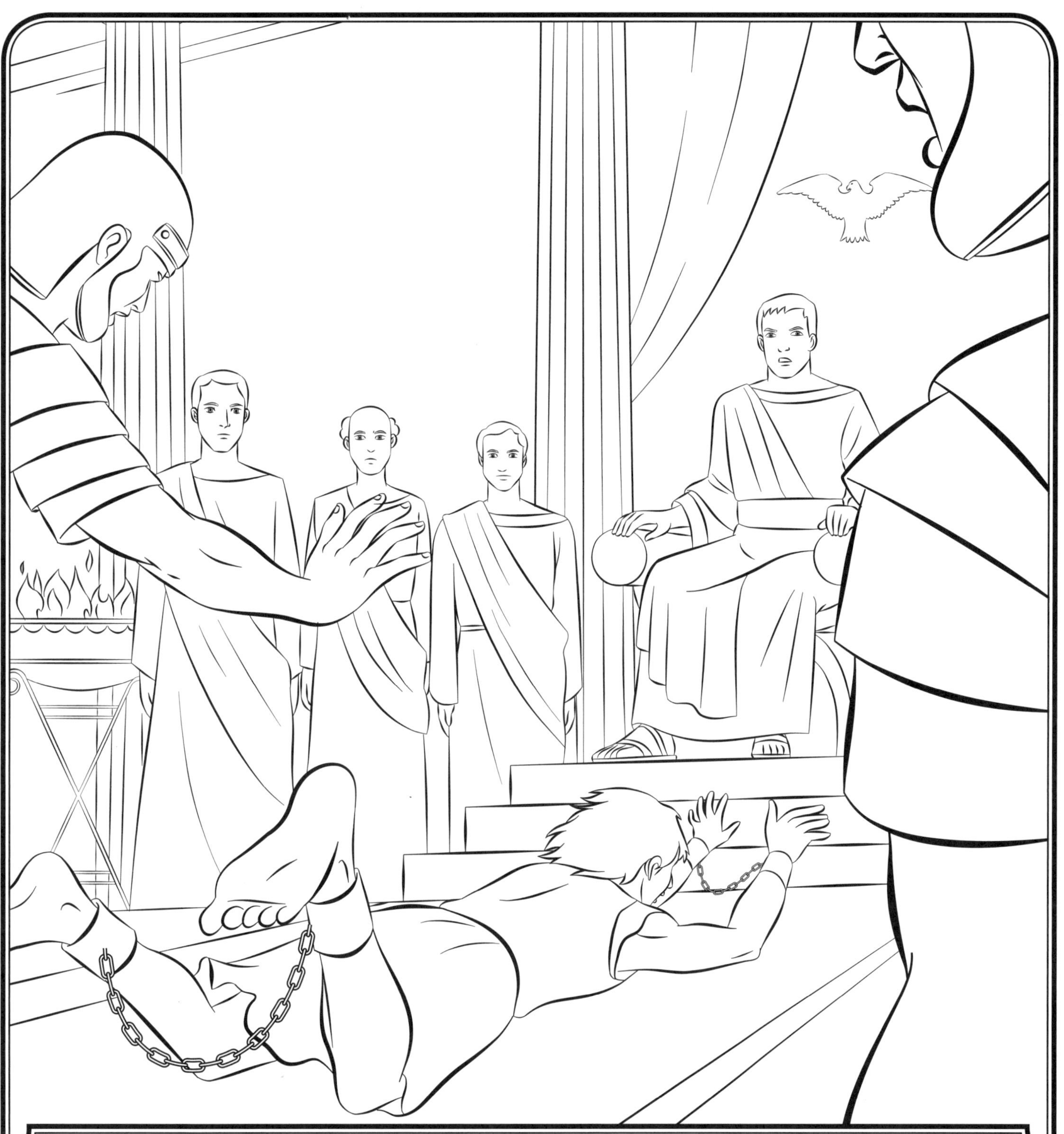

Before long, Valentinus had been found. He was put in heavy chains and brought before the emperor and members of the court.

“What is this that I have heard?” asked the emperor. “Why are you disobeying my orders? Don’t you know I can punish you harshly?”

Everyone watched Valentinus, expecting him to fall to his knees and beg for mercy. Instead, Valentinus boldly explained to the emperor how marriage was God's idea. "Marriage is a blessing from God," he said. And then he went on to tell the emperor all about his Christian faith.

Valentinus was so sincere that the emperor almost converted to Christianity. Sadly, however, he was very angry that Valentinus had disobeyed him. His pride got the best of him and he ordered that Valentinus be killed.

Poor Valentinus was thrown into a very dark and lonely prison. But instead of feeling sorry for himself, he began to pray for the people of Rome and even for the emperor himself.

Marcus, the jailer, stopped to watch the brave priest. "How could Valentinus think of others at a time like this?" he wondered.

Many days later, Valentinus saw that Marcus looked quite sad. “What is the matter?” Valentinus asked.

“Its my little daughter. She has been blind since birth and it hurts me to see her struggle,” sighed Marcus.

“I will pray for her,” replied the good priest. “With God nothing is impossible.”

The very next day, Valentinus' prayers were interrupted when Marcus ran to his cell. "My daughter," exclaimed the smiling jailer. "She can see! It's a miracle! Jesus healed my daughter."

Valentinus rejoiced along with Marcus. Soon the jailer and his family decided to become Christians!

Valentinus taught Marcus and his family all about Christ. He made friends with them and wrote them letters telling them about God's love and signed them, "Your Valentinus".

Valentinus continued to be a brave example of his faith until the day of his execution. He knew he had done his best to obey God. He knelt before the soldier with the drawn sword and prayed again for the people of Rome.

He died on February 14, 270 AD.

In 496, Pope Gelasius I made February 14 a feast day in honor of Saint Valentine. His custom of sending letters to others and signing them, "Your Valentinus" soon turned into a custom for many people.